LIFE SKILLS

CRAFTY CREATIVITY

Sue Barraclough

Heinemann Library
Chicago, Illinois

www.heinemannraintree.com
Visit our website to find out
more information about
Heinemann-Raintree books.

To order:
☎ Phone 888-454-2279
🖳 Visit www.heinemannraintree.com
   to browse our catalog and order online.

© 2009 Heinemann Library
an imprint of Capstone Global Library, LLC
Chicago, Illinois

Customer Service: 888-454-2279

Visit our website at
www.heinemannraintree.com

Edited by Harriet Milles and Adam Miller
Designed by Philippa Jenkins and Artisitix
Original illustrations © Capstone Global Library
    Limited 2008
Illustrated by KJA Artists
Picture research by Elizabeth Alexander

Printed and bound in China by South China
    Printing Company Ltd.

13 12 11 10 09
10 9 8 7 6 5 4 3 2 1

**Library of Congress Cataloging-in-Publication
Data**

Barraclough, Sue.
  Crafty creativity / Sue Barraclough. -- 1st ed.
    p. cm. -- (Life skills)
  Includes bibliographical references and index.
  ISBN 978-1-4329-2720-2 (hc)
  1. Handicraft. I. Title.
  TT157.B339 2009
  745.5--dc22
                    2008047815

Acknowledgments
The author and publishers are grateful to
the following for permission to reproduce
copyright material: © Alamy/Bob Elam p. **16**;
© Alamy/Elizabeth Whiting & Associates p. **37**;
© Capstone Global Library pp. **9, 40** bottom,
45, 47; © Capstone Global Library/MM Studios
pp. **11, 20, 21, 22** top, **22** bottom, **23, 25, 27, 29,
30, 32, 42, 46** top, **46** bottom; © Getty Images
pp. **48** (Robert Harding World Imagery), **12**
(Taxi/Lee Strickland); © Istockphoto/Rick Rhay
p. **36** left; © Photolibrary/Photographic Dan
Gair/Index Stock Imagery p. **4**; © Rex Features/
Paul Cooper p. **39**; © Shutterstock pp. **34** (Amy
Walters), **40** top (David Hsu), **34** (Fritz Kocher),
7 (Jan Hopgood), **36** top (Mary E. McCabe), **45**
(Stephen Coburn), **34** (Victoria Alexandrova),
34 (ViZualStudio) **40** bottom (Yuri Arcurs),
28, 36 right; © Topham Picturepoint/Bob
Daemmrich p. **15**.

Cover photograph of a young woman holding
giant knitting needles reproduced with
permission of © Corbis/Cultura.

The cards featured on page 42 were made by
Sarah Shannon.

We would like to thank Joanna Hinton-Malivoire
and Katie Miller for their invaluable help in the
preparation of this book.

Every effort has been made to contact copyright
holders of material reproduced in this book.
Any omissions will be rectified in subsequent
printings if notice is given to the publishers.

Contents

Some words are printed in bold, **like this**. You can find out
what they mean by looking in the glossary.

WHAT IS A CRAFT?

A craft is making something useful or decorative by hand, using simple tools. Most crafts require specific skills and techniques, equipment, and often materials to create a particular product. Unlike items made in huge quantities by factory machines, something made by hand is unique.

CRAFT SKILLS

This book will teach you simple skills for a mix of crafts. It is a brief introduction to the world of crafts and should help you find out which types of craft appeal to you. The aim is to aid understanding of skills, materials, and terminology, as well as to provide ideas and inspiration. Hopefully, you will then want to find out more and develop your own designs and ways of working.

Different by design

Each craft has a set of instructions or a series of steps to follow in order to make something. Each person follows the instructions to make a similar product. The great thing is that each person can follow the same steps and make small changes to create something unique. Once you are confident about what you are doing, you can make more changes to create something new and different.

Traditional crafts create useful and beautiful items using skills passed down through the generations.

Getting it Right

A skilled craftsperson or **artisan** uses the right tools, and uses them safely and well. A crucial part of every craft is choosing the best tools for the job.

Ideas and inspiration

For any craft, having a collection of ideas and styles is inspiring. Collect beads, fabrics, printed papers, or pictures from magazines, and add them to a poster board or a large notebook so you will never be short of inspiration. Some things to remember:

- Keep an open mind. Experiment, think, plan, doodle, and play around with ideas.

- Ideas or skills you have learned for one craft may be useful for another. For example, you might use embroidery stitches on a piece of knitting or a string of beads to decorate a fabric bag.

- Keep pictures and sketches of anything you like; you don't need to know how you will use them. Seeing how other people have used materials and color will help you decide what you think works.

Color in crafts

Choosing colors that work together is not always easy, so understanding how a color wheel works helps. **Primary colors** are red, yellow, and blue. **Secondary colors** are made by mixing primary colors together. On a color wheel, similar colors are side by side, and different colors are opposite each other. Looking at colors in nature is a useful way to see how colors can be combined. For example, the reds and oranges of a sunset are similar colors. But the red of a tulip and its green stem and leaves are **complementary** colors that are opposite each other on the color wheel. Understanding color similarities and differences is the key to making color choices.

A color wheel is a handy tool when choosing color combinations.

5

Needlecraft

Sewing is an important life skill. Whether you need to sew on a button or mend a favorite shirt, there won't always be someone around to do it for you. Some simple sewing skills will also mean you can try some cool **customizing** projects.

CUSTOMIZING YOUR CLOTHES

Fashions change all the time, so having the sewing skills to adapt your clothes to stay with the trends, and to look good on you, can only be a good thing. Color, fabrics, and decorative details can all be used to update clothes and keep your wardrobe cool. Study fashion magazines to see how different designers use color, texture, patterns, and other details in their clothes.

Finding your own style

Understanding how clothes are made and learning about different fabrics is crucial to finding your own style. Thrift stores are full of cheap clothes for you to experiment with. If you decide you do not like the end result, at least you have still given money to a good cause.

Storing sewing equipment

Bu keeping your sewing supplies organized, you will make sewing more fun. If your sewing basket is a pile of knotted threads and jumbled fabrics, you will never be able to find anything. The best sewing basket is one where you can find things quickly, so that you can move forward with the challenge of creating something.

Try to create a separate compartment or drawer for storing interesting items that you may have collected over time. You are more likely to feel motivated if your sewing kit is filled with inspirational odds and ends.

> **TIP**
>
> Before you throw away old clothes, save any beautiful buttons and scraps of fabric. Also keep favorite lace trimmings or other decorative items, as you may be able to use them again in unexpected ways. The clever use of unusual buttons or trim can often transform a boring item into something beautiful and unique.

Pincushion

Use two contrasting colored, textured, or patterned fabrics, but make sure the fabrics are a similar thickness. Put a small bowl or a saucer on the pieces of fabric and draw around them to make two circles. Cut out the fabric circles. Put the right sides together and sew a half-inch (1.3-centimeter) seam all the way around, leaving 1 inch (2.5 centimeters) open. Turn so the right sides show, and stuff the cushion shape with cotton balls or **batting**. Sew up the gap. Decorate with stitches, buttons, or sequins.

Needle book

Make a needle book for storing your needles by cutting out a rectangle of felt. Fold it in half like a book. Then cut out three or four slightly smaller rectangles of a thinner fabric to make the "pages" of the book. Put the pages inside the felt cover, and use a large needle and yarn to sew three or four stitches to hold the pages in. You could knit a cover for this as a simple knitting project (see page 19).

Sewing kit basics

A sewing kit needs a few essential items:

- A package of needles in various sizes
- Cotton thread—black and white are the most useful
- Dressmaking shears or sharp scissors

- A tape measure
- A box of straight pins
- Hooks, eyes, and snaps
- Buttons
- Safety pins
- A thimble for pushing needles through thick fabric.

Sewing stitches

Learning a few simple stitches will help you tackle most sewing tasks. However, if you want to add decoration to your project, you can teach yourself some basic embroidery stitches. Embroidery is using decorative stitching to create pictures or patterns.

Embroidery stitches

stem stitch—use to make an outline for items or patterns on fabric

appliqué stitch—use for sewing on patches of material. Keep the stitches close to raw edges to stop them from fraying.

chain stitch—a series of loops for borders or flower stems

knot stitch—a simple stitch that adds dots of color

lazy daisy—for simple flower and petal shapes

satin stitch—a versatile stitch that can be adapted to create many different designs

Useful stitches

hemming stitch—use for shortening skirts and pants so that the stitches don't show

back stitch—use to sew fabric firmly together, or to make bold or thin lines

slip stitch—use to make an invisible seam between two folded edges

running stitch—a series of short stitches that can be used for hems or seams. You can also use it to add simple decorative details.

blanket stitch—ideal for sewing along the edge of fabrics to stop them from fraying

basting stitch—use to temporarily hold pieces of fabric together

Sewing on buttons

Sometimes cheap or dull buttons can make a garment seem boring, but you can often transform it simply by sewing on new buttons:

1. Close the garment so you can mark the position of the buttons. If you are replacing buttons, cut the old ones off, leaving a thread behind to mark their position.

2. Thread your needle with a piece of thread matching the button and make a knot in the end.

3. Push the needle through the first hole in the button and then back through the next. Sew in and out of the holes at least six or seven times.

4. Wind the thread around and around under the button a few times.

5. Push the needle back through to the back of the button and knot.

Don't be tempted **TIP** to make your thread too long. It will just get tangled and knotted as you try to pull it through the fabric you are sewing. You may think that a long thread will save you time, but it won't!

Simple brooch

Sew a simple brooch. Roughly cut out a flower or other **graphic** element from a piece of thick fabric (such as curtain fabric). Glue the flower shape to felt and cut carefully around the edges. Stitch around the edge using the blanket stitch.

You can also stitch on beads or sequins, or sew some simple stitches such as knot stitches. Glue to a brooch fastening or even a safety pin. (A small patch of fabric glued over the back of the pin will hold it in place.)

TRANSFORMING T-SHIRTS

If you have an old T-shirt with a graphic or design that you love and are sorry to lose, save it! Simply cut out the design and transfer it to a brand new T-shirt. Cheap department stores sell plain T-shirts that you can transform.

New life for an old T-shirt

You will need:

- A plain T-shirt
- A design or graphic you want to use again
- Fabric glue
- Pins and scissors
- A needle and colored thread.

T-shirt surgery

Cut out the picture or decoration you want to save from the old T-shirt, making sure you leave a border of about ¼ inch (0.6 centimeters) around it. Position it on the new T-shirt, and hold it in place with a pin or fabric glue. Sew the blanket stitch in a contrasting thread all the way around the patch.

Inside-out patch

For an interesting variation, you could cut out the design or decoration, leaving a ½-inch (1.3-centimeter) border around it. Think about where you want the design to be on the new T-shirt. Then pinch a piece of fabric right in the middle of this area and cut a small hole. Put the piece of material underneath the T-shirt so you can see the center of the design through the hole. Use a pin to hold the material there. Then turn the T-shirt inside out. Use more pins to secure the material firmly in place while you sew around the edge.

Turn the T-shirt the right way around again. Carefully cut away the material using the small hole as your starting point, leaving about ¼ inch (0.6 centimeters) of material to frame the new image.

QUICK CRAFT

Tie-dye

To give an old T-shirt a retro, "hippie" look, try the tie-dye effect. First, lay the shirt out flat on a table or work surface. Pinch the center, and lift it slowly upward. Run your other hand down the T-shirt, gathering it together in folds. Tightly wind a rubber band around the shirt, about 2 in. (5 cm) from the top. Add more rubber bands down the length of the T-shirt, spaced roughly 2 in. (5 cm) apart. Soak the T-shirt in a fabric dye for about 20 minutes. Wearing protective gloves, remove the T-shirt from the dye, remove the rubber bands, rinse, and dry. Visit http://crafts.kaboose.com/tie-dyeing.html for more great tie-dye ideas.

Other simple ideas for customizing shirts:
- Sew crystals or sequins along the neck or the straps of a tank top.
- Sew beads or sequins on flowers or other graphics to add interest and texture.
- Dye white cotton T-shirts in bright colors. Try **tie-dye** (see box on page 10) or **batik** patterns.
- Make longer sleeves into cap sleeves by cutting and hemming.

Stitching on a row of colorful beads is another quick and easy way to transform an old T-shirt.

USING A SEWING MACHINE

If you own or can borrow a sewing machine, there are other sewing projects you can try. You will be able to make things much faster using a sewing machine. It is possible to do most simple projects on a machine that does only a simple straight stitch—you don't need a fancy machine!

How a sewing machine works

It is a good idea to understand how a sewing machine works so that you can get the most out of it. Basically, the needle pushes the thread through the fabric, catching a second thread from a **bobbin** under the "throat plate" in the base of the machine. This loops the two threads together to form a strong stitch.

Practicing skills

Practice using the different stitches on your machine on scraps of material. Try sewing in straight lines and then see if you can curve the stitches around in a smooth line. Don't start sewing your actual clothing until you feel you are in control of the machine.

Threading a sewing machine can be challenging, but practice makes perfect!

Getting it Right

Make sure you read the manual carefully before you begin to use a new sewing machine. Pay close attention to any safety instructions. Before you start any project, test a small piece of the fabric you are using first to make sure you get the tension (the tightness of the stitches) right. Use a sharp needle and good quality thread for each project.

Quick and easy bag

You will need:
35 in. (90 cm) of thick fabric, such as denim, canvas, or upholstery, matching thread, scissors, and a tape measure

sew

fold

sew

❶ For the bag, measure and cut a long rectangle 30 by 12 in. (76 by 30 cm). For the handles, measure and cut two more rectangles 20 by 6 in. (51 by 15 cm).

❸ To make the bag, sew a ½-in. (1.3-cm) seam along the short ends of the rectangle. Sew the handles about 3 in. (7.6 cm) in from the edges on the seam.

fold

fold

fold

❷ To make the handles, fold the long edges of the rectangle into the middle, then fold the whole thing in half. Pin and sew together along the long open edge.

❹ Fold the rectangle in half with the good sides together and sew down the two long sides. Turn the bag the right way out, and your bag is ready to use.

13

MASTERING SKILLS

Begin by sewing very simple pieces such as bags or cushion covers. If you rush out to buy complicated patterns and expensive fabrics before you have mastered the basics, you may have problems and waste your time and materials. As a beginner, choose projects that are quick and easy to finish. These will give you a sense of achievement and build up your confidence. To fine-tune your skills, practice making simple items as gifts for friends. If you experiment with different materials and fabrics, you will learn what works by trial and error.

Getting ideas

If you have access to the Internet, you will find hundreds of websites featuring ideas and inspiration (and even patterns to print out and use) for all sorts of cool stuff. If you take the time to plan and research ideas, you will be more likely to make something spectacular that you will want to use or wear all the time.

Picking the right fabrics

If you are choosing clothes from a thrift store to customize, it is worth checking the labels to find out what materials they are made from. Clothes made from natural fabrics such as **silk**, cotton, **linen**, and wool will wash and wear well. **Artificial** fabrics look great when they are new, but will tend to sag and fade after a few washes.

Getting it Wrong

The position or **proportion** of decorative details is essential for the success of your design. If you add big, heavy buttons to a tiny T-shirt, the material will just sag. If you add tiny sequins where they cannot be seen, you'll have wasted your time. Think carefully about the decorations you add.

When choosing fabrics, remember that some materials are easier to work with than others. Silks can be slippery and hard to handle. Leather needs special needles and very strong thread. For beginners, cotton is cheaper and easier to work with.

Quilting and other sewing crafts

Quilting is a very popular craft. It is a form of patchwork, using three layers of fabric: the top layer, which is usually made up of pieces of fabric sewn together to form a pattern; the middle layer, which is soft padding material; and the bottom layer, which is usually plain. Quilting is stitching the layers together, and it can be done by hand or by machine.

Wearing a thimble while you sew your quilt makes pushing the needle through layers of fabric much less painful!

15

YARN CRAFT

Yarn is a long, strong thread that is formed by spinning and twisting fibers such as wool, cotton, fur, or even acrylics. The yarn can be knitted to make sweaters, hats, scarves, gloves, and a whole range of accessories. Knitting uses two needles to loop and weave the yarn together.

KNITTING TO GO

The great thing about knitting is that you can do it anywhere. Once you have mastered the basics, you can knit while you travel on a bus or train, in a waiting room, or while you watch TV.

Knitting needles

Knitting needles are usually made from metal, wood, or plastic. The pointed end is the knitting part and the knob on the end stops the knitting from slipping off. Needles come in different sizes, and the size relates to how thick they are, size 0 (2mm) being the thinnest. Thicker needles create bigger stitches. It is important to use the right size needles if you are following a pattern, otherwise your finished garment will not fit you.

Most knitters find the knitting process calming and relaxing.

Useful knitting tools

- *A row counter*—this helps count how many rows you have knitted

- *Needle guards*—when you put knitting away, they stop stitches from falling off and also stop the needles from sticking into you. You can use old bottle corks.

- *Small sharp scissors*—for cutting yarn and trimming loose ends

- *Darning or tapestry needles*—use these large needles to sew pieces of knitting together

- *Tape measure*—use this for checking sizes and knitting tension (tightness)

- *A crochet hook*—for adding fringes

- *A bag with handles*—to fit your yarn, needles, pattern, and other equipment.

Types of yarn

Visit the yarn section in a store and you will be amazed by the variety of colors and textures. There are **natural fibers**, such as wool, mohair, cotton, silk, and linen, and these are often **blended** or mixed together to create different textures. Wool, which is the most widely used yarn, is made from sheep's wool. Other yarns, such as cashmere, mohair, and angora, are made from goat's wool.

There are also new eco-friendly yarns, such as banana silk yarn, made from the stalks and leaves of banana plants, as well as yarns made from bamboo.

Artificial yarns are usually cheaper. These yarns are made from materials such as acrylic and viscose. Artificial yarns may be blended with natural fibers to make them softer.

A ball of yarn usually has a label that says what the yarn is made of and whether it is natural or artificial fibers. It usually gives washing instructions, the size of needles to use, the color or shade, and lots of other useful information.

HOW TO KNIT

There are two simple stitches to master first: the knit stitch and the purl stitch. Before you can try either of them, however, you need to know how to knit the first row of stitches, which is called casting on.

Casting on

1 Wind the yarn around your finger to make a loop, and then pull the yarn back through the loop to make a **slip knot**. Slip this "stitch" onto the knitting needle.

2 Hold the needle with the slip knot in your left hand. Put the right needle into the stitch and wind the yarn under and over the needle from right to left.

3 Pull the yarn through the stitch and loop this through and onto the left-hand needle, too.

4 Then put the right needle between the two stitches and wind the yarn around again. Pull the yarn through and slip onto the left needle. Continue doing this until you have the number of stitches you need.

The knit stitch

1 To make a knit stitch, keep the yarn at the back and put the right needle through the first stitch on the left needle. The movement goes left to right, and front to back.

2 Wrap the yarn around the right needle and pull the loop back through the stitch.

3 Slip this new stitch off the left needle and onto the right.

The purl stitch

❶ To make a purl stitch, keep the yarn at the front and put the right needle into the front of the first stitch, going back to front and right to left.

❷ Wrap the yarn around the right needle, and pull the loop through.

❸ Slip the stitch off the left needle and onto the right.

Casting off

❶ Casting off, or binding off, is making a neat edge that will not come undone. Knit two stitches, then using the left-hand needle tip, take the first stitch and lift it over the second stitch.

❷ Then slide if off the needle.

❸ Now knit another stitch and repeat until only one stitch remains on your left-hand needle. Cut your yarn and pass the tail through your last stitch, pulling it tight.

Beginner knitters sometimes make their stitches too tight. At first, try to focus on wrapping the yarn more loosely to make sure this does not happen. New knitters often cast off too tightly, too. It might help to use a slightly bigger needle for casting off. If you are left-handed you probably won't have a problem with these instructions. However, if you do, there are books and lots of websites with clear instructions and hints and tips for the left-handed knitter.

TIP

KNITTING A SCARF

A scarf is another perfect project for a novice (beginner) knitter. It allows you to practice knit and purl stitches. By making scarves for your friends, you will gain even more practice. If you cannot find the yarn listed in the pattern, ask for help in your local fabric or craft store, and they should be able to recommend a similar type of yarn for you to use.

If you notice you have dropped a stitch, don't panic and unravel it all. Just go back as far as the dropped stitch and start again. There are many ways to pick up a dropped stitch; check in a knitting book or on the Internet to find out how.

This hat and scarf set is an easy project for a beginner.

→

THE SCARF PATTERN

You will need:

Size 17 knitting needles, 2 balls of Sirdar®
Denim Ultra yarn (use the rest for the hat
on page 22).

- Cast on 12 stitches
- Rows 1-6—knit
- Row 7—purl*
- Row 8—knit
- Repeat last two rows once
- Row 11—knit
- Repeat last row five times**
- Rows 7 to 16 create the pattern
  and repeat * to ** 13 times.
- Next row—knit
- Repeat last row five times
- Cast off

The asterisk (*) in a pattern is used
to indicate rows of knitting that
need to be repeated.

Learning to knit evenly

While you are learning to knit, focus
on trying to knit evenly. If you don't
knit evenly, your knitting will look
lumpy and bumpy. The stitches need
to be just loose enough that you can
push the needle into the loop easily.

When you are starting out, it is a good
idea to count your stitches at the
end of each row to check that you
have not dropped one. This is good
practice, because when you try more
complicated patterns, keeping track
of stitches and rows is a key skill.

Decorative details

Once you have made your scarf, you
might want to add extra decorative
details such as a fringe. Adding
a fringe is easy to do. Use either
the same color yarn or go for a
complementary color. Take four or five
pieces of yarn each measuring about
6 inches (15 centimeters) long and
fold them in half. Use a crochet hook
to pull the yarn through the last row
of knitting stitches to make a loop.
Pull the ends through the loop and
pull tight.

KNITTING A HAT

Once you have practiced your knitting skills by making some scarves, you can move on to something more challenging. This is a simple hat to make, because once you have knitted the pattern, you simply sew up one seam.

In this pattern, you knit two stitches together, which is shortened to "k2tog." This is a way to shape your knitting. To do this, you simply put the right needle into two stitches and knit them as if they are one stitch.

THE HAT PATTERN

You will need:

Size 11 needles, Sirdar® Denim Ultra yarn

QUICK CRAFT

- Cast on 51 stitches. "K" means "knit" and "p" means "purl."
- Row 1–8—knit
- Row 9—knit
- Row 10—purl
- Repeat last two rows six times
- Row 23—(k3, k2tog) 10 times, k1
- 41 stitches
- Row 24—purl
- Row 25—(k2, k2tog) 10 times, k1
- 31 stitches
- Row 26—purl
- Row 27—(k1, k2tog) 10 times, k1
- 21 stitches
- Row 27—purl
- Row 28—(k2tog) 10 times, k1
- 11 stitches
- Row 29—purl
- Cast off

To finish, sew the side seams together. Use a darning needle and matching yarn. Sew along the seam using a neat overstitch. Sew the yarn in at the end of the seam and knot.

A FLOWER PATTERN

Try knitting a simple flower to decorate your hat.

You will need:
Size 11 needles, yarn (you could use the same yarn as for the hat and scarf, but any yarn and appropriate-sized needle works), tapestry or darning needle

There is only one row to this flower after casting on.

- Cast on 40 stitches
- Knit 1, cast off six stitches (you now have two stitches on your right needle)
- K1, cast off six stitches (you now have four stitches on your right needle)
- K1, cast off six stitches (you now have six stitches on your right needle)
- K1, cast off six stitches (you now have eight stitches on your right needle)
- K1, cast off six stitches (you now have 10 stitches on your right needle)
- Cut the yarn about 8 inches (20 centimeters) from the knitting. Thread the 8-inch (20-centimeter) tail through a tapestry needle and pull that needle through each of the remaining 10 stitches on your needle from the first to the last knitted. Remove the stitches from the needle and pull tightly. Secure the ends by sewing and knotting at the back of the flower.

It's important to get the tension (tightness) of your knitting right, so that your hat is the right size. It is easy to get so involved with following a pattern that you knit too tightly. If you do this you may find that your hat is too small!

Getting it Right

23

DEVELOPING YOUR SKILLS

Once you have learned the basics, there are books and websites giving ideas and instructions for other projects for beginner knitters. You may find a local group that provides workshops or simply gets together to knit. This is a fun way to get advice and inspiration from more experienced knitters.

TRY THIS!

Felting is a fun thing to do with your knitting. You wash the knitted item in hot water and it will shrink and look like felt. You need to use 100 percent wool yarn. Experiment with small knitted squares to start with. Look for books about felting at the library or search for information on felting on the Internet.

Following a pattern

In most patterns words will be shortened. For example:

- "St" means "stitch."
- "Cont" means "continue."
- "Rep" means "repeat."

Don't worry if this is hard to understand at first. You will soon get used to it.

There are many new words to learn, and here are some of the most common:

- "Tension" (also known as gauge) is how many stitches and rows you should have for every 1 inch (2.5 centimeters) you knit. It is a good idea when using more complex patterns to knit a sample to test that the size is correct.

- "Increase" (shortened to "inc") is adding a new stitch to a row to make it longer.

- "Decrease" ("dec") is taking a stitch from a row to make it shorter.

- "Garter stitch" is knitting every row.

- "Stocking stitch" is knitting one row and purling the next.

As you learn to knit, you will discover new words and understand what other knitters are talking about!

As you knit, mark where you are on the pattern, so that you do not lose track. If you put your knitting down, it is easy to forget which direction you were knitting, so try to finish a row before you answer the door or the phone.

TIP

Crochet craft

A crochet hook is a useful knitting tool, and knowing some simple crochet stitches can be handy. Crochet uses one hooked needle to make the stitches.

Crochet is a great to way to make fancy edges for knitting and other decorative pieces. Turn to page 52 to find details of a website that has clear videos of all the stitches. There are also books you can use to teach you to crochet. Learn how to do single and double crochet. Practice until you are confident you can crochet each stitch well.

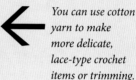

You can use cotton yarn to make more delicate, lace-type crochet items or trimming.

Crochet flower

QUICK CRAFT

Use chunky yarn and a large hook (size L/11) to make a crochet flower.
["Sc" means "single crochet." "Dc" means "double crochet."]

Make a chain of 20 stitches. Sc into 3rd chain from hook. Then sc, dc, sc, sc all in the same stitch. Sc into next chain. Then sc, dc, sc, sc into same stitch, sc into next, and so on to the end of the chain.

Finish off, leaving about 12 inches (30 centimeters) of free yarn. Pull the yarn through the last loop and knot. Roll up from one end to form a flower shape. Thread a darning needle onto the long piece of yarn, and then thread the yarn through the bottom of the flower (chain side) and pull tight, gathering in the bottom. Tie off. Decorate the center of the flower with a button or bead.

Jewelry Craft

Jewelry includes decorative pieces such as necklaces, bracelets, rings, and earrings. Many techniques are used in jewelry making, some using precious metals such as gold and silver and also expensive gemstones. You can make your own jewelry using beautiful beads and wire or stringing materials. Making jewelry is versatile, creative, and fun.

A Brief History of Beads

Beads have been used all over the world for thousands of years. At first beads would have been crafted from materials such as shell, bone, or wood. In many cultures, beads are used to give information about the wearers—for instance, to show if they are married or their status in a tribe.

DID YOU KNOW?

At one time in Africa and the Americas, beads were used by European traders as currency.

Types of bead

Beads can be beautiful and **versatile**. There are hundreds of sizes, styles, colors, and shapes. How beads look (the finish) can also vary. Some beads are carved and textured, while others are smooth. Some beads are transparent and some are **opaque**. Some beads have **iridescent** finishes that make them shiny like metal.

Beads are made of many different materials such as plastic, wood, metals such as tin, gold, and silver, ceramic, glass, or **semi-precious stones**.

Using different beads

By experimenting you will learn how different beads can be combined together. A beginner can learn a lot by simply threading different beads on a stringing material.

A simple necklace of beads all in the same size and color can be beautiful. However, you may find that the beads sit better with "spacer" beads between them. Spacers are narrow beads that are either plain or have simple designs. By placing spacer beads between more fancy ones, you can make the more eye-catching beads stand out.

Experiment with patterns of beads, such as three of one type and four of another, and mix beads of different materials and shapes. Alternatively, you could try randomly threading a mixture of glass beads onto a string just to see how they turn out.

When you go to a bead store, take time to feel and weigh the different materials. Glass and metal beads are generally heavier than beads made of wood or plastic. The weight of the beads is important when designing a piece of jewelry. Sometimes you need heavy beads to make a necklace hang well, but earrings made of heavy beads are uncomfortable to wear.

Beads come in a fabulous range of sizes, shapes, materials, and colors.

MAKING JEWELRY

You can buy jewelry kits that contain all you need to make a piece of jewelry. These kits are good for a beginner, but nothing beats choosing beads and deciding how to use them. You may be surprised how easy it is to design a simple piece from scratch.

Some striking pieces of jewelry are made from everyday objects. Some designers use ordinary household items such as safety pins and buttons to create fabulous pieces.

Different findings

"Findings" are metal pieces that hold jewelry together or in place, such as necklace clasps, earring wires, brooch backs, jump rings, and crimp beads.

- *Jump rings* are simple rings that can be opened and used to join things together.

- *Crimp beads* are soft metal beads that can be crushed, using a special tool, to secure other beads.

- *Head pins* are pieces of wire with a flat end to stop the bead from falling off. They can be used to make dangle earrings and pendants.

- *Earring wires* are small pieces of wire that have been formed to fit through pierced-ear holes and fasten securely.

If you are choosing earring wires, avoid the brass or plated ones, as they can cause ear infections. Pay more for surgical steel or silver ones if you can.

Learn by looking at the jewelry in your home or in a store and studying how different findings have been used.

Look and learn

It is important to use the right findings. The more knowledge you have, the more likely you are to make the right choices. Hunt out pieces of jewelry and different beads in thrift stores. You can see how jewelry is made by taking it apart and then reusing the beads and other parts to make new pieces.

Getting it Right

Make sure the beads you choose to use have a big enough hole so you can thread them. Imagine how annoyed you would be if you bought beautiful beads and found they were useless for your piece!

Make a simple "lariat" necklace

QUICK CRAFT

Buy a piece of thin leather cord about 24 inches (61 centimeters) long. You will need two large beads and ten smaller beads.

Make a knot about ¼ inch (6 centimeters) from one end, then thread on a large bead and make another knot to hold it in place.

Make another knot about 2 inches (5 centimeters) along and add another smaller bead and knot that in place, too.

String and knot the rest of the beads, adding the larger bead to finish.

Wear this lariat necklace by simply tying it loosely around your neck.

WIRE AND BEAD JEWELRY

Creating jewelry with beads and wire is fairly easy to do and requires only a few tools. There are some simple techniques to learn, and then you can start experimenting.

Essential tools

- *A board*—use for cutting and gluing. This could be a piece of wood or an old chopping board.

- *A bead mat*—cheap to buy and made of special material that stops beads from rolling away as you work. A good alternative is a towel.

- *Pliers*—the most useful for a beginner are round-nose and chain-nose pliers. Buy the best you can afford.

- *Side cutters*—it is best to buy real jewelry cutters, because they are smaller and allow you to trim wire more neatly.

- *Plastic storage boxes*—clear boxes save you from rummaging through containers to find beads.

Check prices on the Internet, but if you buy from a local craft store you can try out different equipment to make sure it works for you.

Getting it Right

Always use safety goggles when you are cutting wire. The pieces of wire can fly off as they are cut and could easily hit you in the eye. You can buy safety goggles cheaply from a craft store. Always hold the end of the wire you are cutting to prevent it from flying off.

round-nose pliers

chain-nose pliers

side cutters

Choosing wire

Start with 18- to 20-gauge wire. The best wire for a beginner is brass. It is cheap and sold in large coils. This means you can get plenty of practice. Memory wire is another useful material to experiment with. It is called memory wire because it is coiled into circles and keeps this shape. You can buy memory wire in sizes suitable for necklaces, bracelets, and rings.

Wire wrapping

One of the simplest and most useful techniques you can learn is wire wrapping. To practice this you will need a straight pin, a bead, and pliers.

❶ Thread a bead onto the pin. Use your round-nose pliers to grip the wire just above the bead. Push the wire with your finger, and bend it to a 90° angle.

❷ Using your round-nose pliers, grip the wire just above the bend.

❸ Then wrap the wire around the pliers until it is pointing down.

❹ Wind the wire around the wire at the top of the bead to make a loop. Hold the loop in the pliers and wrap the wire around the pin, wrapping away from you.

❺ Snip off the extra wire as close to the bead as you can. Squeeze the wrapped wire gently with your chain-nose pliers to make sure the wire end does not stick out.

MAKING NECKLACES AND EARRINGS

This page will give you ideas about how to make pieces of jewelry using some of the techniques you have learned. Don't feel you have to copy anything exactly—unless you want to, of course! You can always add extra beads or use different findings to make the pieces your own.

You will need:

- Earring wires
- Straight pins
- Jump rings
- A selection of beads
- Stringing material
- Clasps.

Add more beads

Add a mixture of beads to your pin, to make dangle earrings. To make simpler earrings, you can just make a loop above the bead, making sure the end of the wire folds snugly back to the bead. This is similar to the wire-wrapping technique, but you do not wrap the wire.

Making a wire-wrapped necklace

Use the wire-wrapping technique from page 31 to make a pendant necklace. Choose a large bead and think about adding smaller beads above it on the pin.

Then choose your stringing material. You could simply string your pendant onto a silver chain, or you could cut a piece of leather cord.

earring wire

straight pin

jump ring

Perfecting techniques

If you want your pieces of jewelry to look neat and professional, you will need to practice your wire-handling techniques. You may find it helpful to practice using the pliers with leftover pieces of wire. Twist the wire in different directions to create coils and loops and form different patterns and shapes. Practice the wire-wrapping procedure over and over until you thoroughly master the skill.

After a while you will become more skilled at using the pliers, and you will find that you become more confident when working with wire.

Learning more

The examples we have shown you in this book cover the simplest forms of jewelry making. Obviously there are many more techniques to learn. One of the best ways to pick up new skills is to decide on a particular item you would like to make, then do some research in books and on the Internet to see if anyone else has done something similar. Most craftspeople are happy to share ideas and give hints and tips on techniques.

Check your local listings or on the Internet to find courses and workshops in your area. These offer great opportunities for swapping ideas, using new tools, learning new skills, and trying out different materials.

TRY THIS!

Using jump rings

Jump rings are useful for joining parts together. Use jump rings to add bead dangles to necklaces. Attach a jump ring to a charm to add the charm to a necklace.

When you open a jump ring, use two pairs of pliers to twist the two ends in opposite directions to open it. Never pull it apart to open the circle, because this will distort the shape, and it will be difficult to restore it.

Paper Craft

Paper is made of plant fibers. The word "paper" comes from the Egyptian word "papyrus." The ancient Egyptians made paper by gluing small pieces of papyrus reed together to form sheets. Today, most paper is made from wood pulp.

Types of Paper

Paper is a great **medium** for crafts because it is cheap, easy to work with, and versatile. Tissue paper, wrapping paper, coated and printed papers, handmade paper, **newsprint**, and **parchment** are all different types of paper.

Feel different pieces of paper between your fingers: some are smooth, some are bumpy, some are flexible, and some are stiff.

The nature of paper

As paper is formed, the fibers line up in parallel. This is called the **grain**. Paper is more flexible along the line of the fibers than across them. Understanding the nature of paper and how it is made will help you when you are using it.

If you tear a piece of paper, you can see the fibers underneath the smooth surface. Try tearing it in different directions to see if it looks different. If you hold any paper up to the light, you can see the texture of the fibers.

Paper-craft tools and equipment

Working with paper requires very few tools. However, it is important to choose good-quality tools. Small, sharp scissors will make all the difference to a paper cut-out. Basic white glue can make some thin papers wrinkle and may ruin a **collage**.

These are the essential tools for working with paper:

- *Scissors*—large scissors are best for cutting large sheets of paper. Use small scissors with pointed blades for cutting out small pictures and shapes.

- *Craft knives*—a good quality knife with a replaceable blade is best. Make sure you change the blade regularly, as a sharp blade is generally safer to use than a blunt one.

- *Cutting mat*—self-healing cutting mats are expensive, but they are designed for the job and make cutting safer because the surface is non-slip. A cheap plastic chopping board is a good alternative.

- *Glue*—Basic white glue is useful for most paper crafts, but it is not ideal for thin papers because it can cause wrinkling. Glue sticks are great for neatly sticking down pieces of paper or thin cardboard, and stronger glues can be useful for adding decorations. A plastic glue spreader can be handy for bigger jobs. Choose glues that are solvent-free.

Getting it Right

If you are using a craft knife, use a metal ruler. A plastic ruler will just get scratched and rough, which will make it useless for other tasks. Always replace your craft knife blade as soon as it becomes blunt. Not only will a sharp blade give you a better cut, but it is also safer because it is less likely to slip around on the paper.

Cutting safely is an important skill when you are using sharp scissors and craft knives. When you are using a craft knife, always cut away from yourself.

DIFFERENT EFFECTS

There are many exciting ways that you can experiment with paper craft just by using different papers that you have at home. For instance you can use old cards, pictures from magazines and newspapers, torn pieces of wrapping paper, and pretty packaging. Old maps and sheet music make great decorative finishes.

Working with papier maché

"Papier maché" is a French term that means "chewed-up paper." A paper pulp is made by tearing paper into small pieces or strips and soaking them with glue. The strips are then stuck together in layers, and they form a material that is a little like a lightweight plaster. If you are using old newspaper, tear the strips rather than cutting them with scissors. This will achieve a smoother surface.

Make a carnival mask

Make a mask by blowing up a balloon so that it is roughly the size of your head. Tear up newspaper strips and soak each strip in a liquid glue solution. Cover one side of the balloon with layers of paper strips; six or seven layers should be enough. Leave to dry and then pop the balloon with a pin.

For a half-face mask, cut out eye holes and a curved shape for the bridge of your nose. For a full-face mask, you can use paper pulp mix—toilet paper is the quickest and easiest to use—to mold features onto your mask. Leave to dry, then paint and varnish. You can decorate your mask with sequins, glitter, or even colored feathers.

QUICK CRAFT

Creating a collage

"Collage" comes from the French verb *coller*, which means "to stick." Collage is gluing pieces of paper or other materials to a piece of cardboard or canvas to create a picture or a piece of art. Materials used can be newspaper clippings, pieces of fabric, colored or handmade papers, or photographs. You can use collage to decorate something ordinary, such as a shoebox, or to make fabulous greetings cards for family and friends.

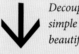

When you are cutting something out, turn the object you are cutting into the scissors whenever possible, rather than turning the scissors.

Decorating with decoupage

"Decoupage" comes from the French word *decouper*, which means "to cut out." Decoupage is a popular and easy way of decorating boxes or items of furniture by carefully cutting out images or patterns from paper (such as floral wrapping paper) and gluing them on. Paint effects are often used to add details. Layers of varnish are then applied to the finished item. The varnish not only provides a tough coating, but also disguises the fact that the images are stuck on. The paper cutouts can look as if they have been carved or painted. A wide range of patterned papers especially for decoupage can be bought in good craft stores or on the Internet.

Decoupage can transform a simple item into something beautiful and unique.

SCRAPBOOKING

Scrapbooking is collecting together photographs and other **memorabilia** into a decorated album. Writing the notes to accompany these items—for instance, funny comments, explanations, dates, or captions—is called journaling.

Planning an ideas scrapbook

An ideal scrapbooking project for a craftsperson is an idea book where you can store all your sources of inspiration. It is a great place to keep interesting pieces of fabric, doodles of designs, newspaper and magazine clippings, and photos. You can also staple resealable bags to some of the pages to store items such as beads, buttons, and lace.

Assembling materials

To start you off, you will need:

- A spiral-bound book with unlined pages
- Resealable bags
- Background papers
- Scissors
- Pencils and pens
- A selection of paints
- Glue, or glue sticks
- A selection of different colored thin cardboard
- Double-sided sticky tape.

Don't crowd too much on each page. If the background is too busy, the photographs get lost. The decorative details should enhance photographs, not distract from them. Add an envelope or a paper pocket to a page to store odds and ends that won't fit on the page.

TIP

Laying out the pages

The first step is to gather all the materials, cuttings, scraps, sketches, doodles, and other odds and ends that you want to keep in your idea book. Some things may look good grouped together by color. Plan some pages as mood boards showing colors, styles, or fashions that you like.

If your ideas scrapbook is for knitting, add yarn samples or pictures of garments or accessories you like. If it is for needlecraft, stick in pictures of projects you would like to make in the future and fabric scraps.

You might want to use your idea book as a record of things you have made so you can look back through and think about what worked well. However, you should also enjoy flipping through it as a source of inspiration.

Planning a scrapbook layout

❶ Buy acid-free papers to preserve photos and other **souvenirs**. Photographs that are kept in an acid-free environment will not fade.

❷ Choose a theme for each page or group of pages. Group photos that show a particular bunch of people or the various stages of an event such as a vacation or an awards presentation.

❸ Decide on the colors that work best with the photos on each page of your album.

❹ Write notes so that you know how much journaling you want to include.

❺ Decide which photos you are going to include on each page. Sort through any other relevant memorabilia such as tickets, postcards, or newspaper clippings that you may want to add.

❼ Crop or trim photos or images to lose anything that is not important. Focus on the subject of each page.

❽ Photos can be mounted using corner mounts, adhesive dots, or acid-free glue. To frame photos, use mats—pieces of thick paper or thin cardboard a little bigger than your photo.

❾ Choose **embellishments** such as stickers, stamps, and rub-ons to decorate your pages.

ORIGAMI

There is some debate about the origins of origami, the ancient art of paper folding. Some people believe that it originally came from China and was taken to Japan, while others think it is of Japanese origin. Origami is usually made using a sheet of square paper, with color or patterns on one side only. There are thousands of different objects and decorative items that can be made simply by folding paper. You can buy books or search the Internet for ideas and instructions on how to create origami objects, from simple paper planes to elaborate sculptures. See page 43 for an origami gift idea.

Origami is the art of transforming square, flat pieces of paper into an endless variety of three-dimensional shapes.

Origami photo frame

If you want to give a photograph to a friend or relative, a few simple origami folds will frame it beautifully for you. Cut a square of wrapping paper. Turn it pattern side down and fold in half, corner to corner one way and then the other. You should have two fold lines diagonally across the paper. Now fold each corner to the middle point and fold back again. Then fold each corner up to the crease made by the previous fold. Finally fold each side up so you have four straight sides. Put a dab of glue on the back of the photograph and position it in the middle of the frame. Add glue to the frame sides and stick them down.

QUICK CRAFT

Saving paper

Save old cards that you like and pictures from magazines, calendars, newspapers, or catalogs. Keep leftover wallpaper, scraps of wrapping paper, stamps, stickers, leaflets, or packaging with interesting designs. Remember that almost anything made from paper can be used and recycled into something new.

When using paper be creative and flexible. Don't feel you have to follow the materials listed for a project exactly. Experiment by choosing a different type or texture of paper or another color. You can create something original and unique by trying out something new. It may not always work out well, but you will learn by experimenting and making mistakes.

Paper beads

You can make beautiful beads from pieces of paper. See the chapter on jewelry making for ideas on how to string your beads.

QUICK CRAFT

❶ Cut or tear strips of paper. Tearing paper will give your beads a more interesting texture.

❷ Wind the paper strip tightly onto a knitting needle or an unfolded paper clip, depending on how big you want the hole to be. Use glue to fix the paper in place. Slide your bead off the paper clip or knitting needle.

❸ Tearing the paper into different shaped strips will produce different shaped beads.

Some Gift Ideas

By making your own gifts, you use your creative craft skills to produce something completely unique. Think about the person you are making the gift for, and of ways you can make it special and personal for him or her. You don't have to spend a lot of money—taking the time and effort to make a homemade gift shows that you care.

The Personal Touch

Making a special and personal gift can be as simple as buying a package of your grandma's favorite tea and putting it in a basket with some homemade cookies wrapped in homemade paper and ribbon. Alternatively, you could buy a package of seeds and paint some small terracotta pots for a friend who loves gardening.

Making cards

Making cards is easy, but you need to make sure that the cards look neat and professional. Use a craft knife, a ruler, and a cutting mat to cut out your rectangle of cardboard, and fold neatly.

The simple cards in the photo on the right were made using thin, colored cardboard, a flower-shaped hole punch (available in good craft stores), some crystals, glue, and colored pens. However, you could try to think up some original card designs of your own:

- Cut letters from magazines and newspapers to spell out a message on the front of your card

- A simple square of beautiful patterned fabric or paper, glued to thin, black cardboard

- A paper pumpkin shape decorated with patterned circles for Halloween

- A house shape decorated with paper pieces for a new home card

- A flower made from a button and paper petals

- A collage card.

Origami gift box

Make this simple origami gift box.

❶ Cut a square piece of colored paper. Fold in half, from top to bottom and half again from side to side, to make two creases.

❷ Using the creases as a guide, fold the four corners into the center.

❸ Using the creases as a guide, fold the top into the center, and the bottom into the center, then unfold to show two creases.

❹ Fold the left and right sides into the center, and unfold to show four creases.

❺ Unfold the top and bottom corners.

❻ Fold up the left and right side.

❼ Push in the corners, and fold down the top into the box.

❽ Repeat with the bottom.

❾ This is your finished box.

Make a slightly bigger box and use it as a lid.

DECORATING PICTURE FRAMES

Take a tired old wooden picture frame and transform it by adding decorative details.

Look for cheap old wooden picture frames at garage sales or thrift stores. Or you may have old frames at home that you can use—but don't forget to check with an adult first! Choose thick, flat frames. If the frames are too thin, or textured, they will be difficult to decorate and will not look so good.

Some picture frame variations:

- Use the collage technique to cover the frame with foil or candy wrappers. Cut the wrappers into small squares. Spread glue on a small section of the frame at a time and overlap the wrapper squares so the frame is covered. Smooth each wrapper carefully for a professional finish.

- Paint the frame with **matte** white paint. Then use a stencil to sponge-print simple shapes around the frame. To make a stencil, cut a simple shape, such as a heart or a circle, out of cardboard. Dip a sponge in paint and dab over the stencil. Move the stencil and repeat.

- Cut out words or phrases that mean something to the person you are giving the frame to. Stick them around the frame and seal them with an acrylic matte varnish.

TRY THIS!

Black and white button frame

You will need:
- **Black gloss paint**
- **Sandpaper**
- **Small white buttons**
- **Plain white glue**
- **Leftover pieces of of thick, brightly colored yarn.**

Clear your work surface and protect it with old newspaper. Collect all the things you need.

Rub the frame with sandpaper to roughen it. Then paint the frame's front and back. Leave the paint to dry for a couple of hours.

Dab a generous glob of glue onto each button and press it onto the frame. Start with one at each corner, and then add three or four down each side.

This simple black and white button frame is striking, but if you want to add some color, trickle swirls of glue between the buttons, and stick pieces of yarn over the swirls.

This frame was made by spreading a layer of glue over a painted wood frame. Shells collected from a beach were pressed into place. Then sand was sprinked on to cover the glue and fill the gaps.

Mats are frames of cardboard used to make sure there is a space between the picture or photograph and the glass. It is a good idea to use a mat, because otherwise the photograph or picture might stick to the glass.

GIFT WRAPPING

An effective way to personalize any gift is to make or customize your own wrapping paper. Alternatively, you could try making simple boxes (see page 47) or customize plain bags to make a gift extra special.

Print it yourself

One of the simplest ways to print paper is to make a potato stamp. First, cut a potato in half. Then draw a simple design on the potato. Cut away the potato around the shape. Paint your shape with colored, acrylic paint and stamp it onto the paper.

Potato printing is a quick and easy way to make your own wrapping paper. Keep the shape simple, and use gold or silver paint for a beautiful finish.

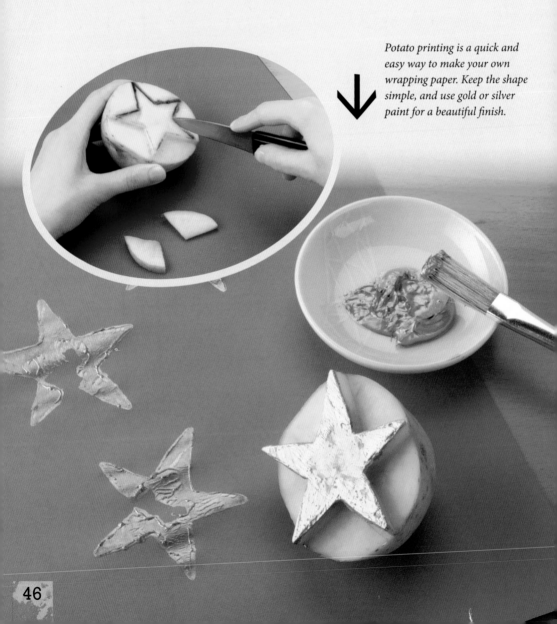

You can also make a stamp by cutting out a shape from a piece of cardboard or a piece of foam or felt. Stick the shape to a small square of wood.

Print your shapes onto plain brown paper, leftover plain wallpaper, graph paper, or sheets of newspaper.

Making gift bags

Plain brown paper bags can be made into cool gift bags. Print a pattern using ideas from the paper-printing section. Or use paper shapes, stickers, sequins, beads, or buttons to decorate the bag.

Gift box

Covering a shoebox or other lidded box with wrapping paper or wallpaper is a quick and effective way to make a gift box.

❶ Place the box lid on the paper and cut around it, leaving about 2 inches (5 centimeters) to spare all the way around.

❷ Fold the paper up two opposite sides first and tape it in place inside the box.

❸ Fold and smooth the paper on the other sides to fit the paper neatly over the box, and tape it in place.

❹ Then cut out paper to fit the box, and cover it in the same way.

To Sum Up

Exploring your creativity through craftwork is fun and rewarding, and it will teach you a range of useful skills. A craft could become a lifelong hobby or you could even turn it into a way of making a living. Many successful craftspeople have started out by making items for friends and family. They then discovered they could sell their work on a larger scale and developed their own small businesses.

DEVELOPING SKILLS

One of the best ways to improve your craft skills is to go to classes and workshops. There you will get an opportunity to exchange ideas with other students, try out new tools, and learn new techniques from experts.

Careers in crafts

Many jobs and careers involve craft skills. For example, if you find that you excel at sewing, you could look toward a career in fashion or theatrical costume design.

Craft for fun!

This book has given you just a brief "taste" of some the crafts you can try. There are many, many others to be explored, such as woodwork, pottery, basket making, weaving, mosaic, metalwork, and ceramics. If you find that knitting or needlework make you feel "all thumbs," then don't worry, there is sure to be another craft that is right for you. Remember, the fun is in the making, so don't be afraid to experiment. Learn from your mistakes—but above all, enjoy yourself!

This beautiful brooch was created by an Egyptian craftsman in 1300 BCE. Visiting museums to look at examples of craftwork is a great way to get ideas and inspiration.

ARE YOU THE CRAFTY TYPE?

1) What is a craft?
a) Making something useful or decorative by hand, using simple tools.
b) Something that is usually frustrating and difficult to do.
c) An activity for a rainy weekend.

2) What do you do when you make a mistake?
a) Scream, blame the tools, and throw it all in the trash.
b) Figure out what went wrong and do it all again more carefully.
c) Continue on and hope no one notices the lumps and bumps.

3) What is a color wheel?
a) A chart showing the relationships between colors.
b) Some sort of design tool.
c) A pretty circle with different colors.

4) How do you usually feel when you finish a piece of craftwork?
a) A little disappointed. It hasn't turned out quite right.
b) Really pleased with it and eager to begin work on something else and learn some new techniques.
c) In a bad mood and tired of bothering with it.

5) If you decide to make a crafty present for a friend, how do you start?
a) Read lots of magazines and study craft websites for ideas. Then spend time planning what to make before you start.
b) Buy a kit that has step-by-step instructions and all the materials you need.
c) Rush out to buy all sorts of expensive tools and materials, then start work right away.

6) How do you finish a piece of craftwork?
a) Somehow you never seem to get around to finishing it. The project lies around the house for weeks and gets forgotten.
b) As neatly as possible, but it is only a present for a friend and he won't mind if it has a frayed edge.
c) Very carefully; the finishing touches can make all the difference.

7) What is the best part about making crafts?
a) You can save money by making cheap gifts.
b) It's a good excuse to buy lots of new equipment.
c) Experimenting and practicing to develop your skills and learn new techniques.

8) What is the most important thing to remember about tools?
a) Pick the right tools for the job and use them safely and well.
b) Buy the most expensive.
c) You can blame them for anything that goes wrong.

ARE YOU THE CRAFTY TYPE?

For page 49

If you chose answer a) score 3.
If you answered b) score 1.
If you answered c) score 2.

2 a) 1 b) 3 c) 2
3 a) 3 b) 2 c) 1
4 a) 1 b) 3 c) 2
5 a) 2 b) 1 c) 3
6 a) 1 b) 2 c) 3
7 a) 2 b) 3 c) 1
8 a) 1 b) 3 c) 2

If you scored between 20 and 24:
Intricate craftwork doesn't hold your interest for long. You tend not to have the patience for the type of craftwork that requires precision and attention to detail. Shopping for materials and tools is usually more appealing than actually making something. This doesn't mean that you are not creative, but you may find you prefer art forms such as painting, sculpture, or woodcarving, where you can express your creativity more freely.

If you scored between 13 and 19:
You enjoy doing crafts from time to time but you are not really interested in learning about crafts in any detail. Crafts are a hobby that is fun and relaxing for rainy days and weekends.

You get pleasure from making things for yourself and other people, and friends and relatives appreciate the time and effort you take to make gifts. You might enjoy developing your skills and learning more, and you could have a hobby that will give you a lifetime of pleasure.

If you scored between 8 and 12:
You may be a skilled craftsperson in the making. You enjoy intricate work and you like to do a good job, no matter how long it takes. This is a useful attribute for a craftsperson, but be careful not to become overly obsessive about tiny details. If you feel crafts might be something you could make a living from, read as much as you can about the crafts that interest you to find out about jobs and careers in related fields. Sign up for workshops and classes so that you can develop your knowledge and improve your techniques.

20 THINGS TO REMEMBER

1. As a beginner, choose quick and easy projects to give you a sense of achievement and build confidence.

2. Remember that making mistakes is part of the learning process.

3. Experiment with different materials and fabrics. You will learn by trial and error what works and what doesn't.

4. If you want your craftwork to look professional, keep practicing your techniques to perfect them.

5. A skilled craftsperson uses the right tools, and uses them safely and well.

6. Preparation and planning are important. Clear a workspace and make sure you have the correct tools at hand.

7. Have a clear plan or design to work from.

8. Keep your mind open to new ideas. Experiment, think, plan, doodle, and play around with ideas.

9. Keep it simple. Simple designs are often the strongest.

10. Save and store pictures and sketches of anything you like; you don't need to know how you will use them.

11. Keep an ideas notebook to inspire you.

12. Make notes on each project to remind you what worked well.

13. Seeing how other people have used materials and color will help you decide what might work for you.

14. Understanding a color wheel and color similarities and differences is important for making color choices.

15. Share ideas with other craftspeople.

16. Go to workshops and classes to exchange ideas and learn from experts.

17. Cutting safely is an important skill when you are using sharp scissors and craft knives. When using a craft knife always cut away from yourself.

18. When you are cutting something out, turn the object you are cutting into the scissors whenever possible, rather than turning the scissors.

19. Always use safety goggles when you are cutting wire.

20. As you knit, always mark where you are on the pattern, so that you do not lose track.

Further Information

BOOKS

Berger, Shoshana. *ReadyMade: How to Make (Almost) Everything*. New York: Clarkson Potter, 2005.

Butler, Amy. *In Stitches: More Than 25 Simple and Stylish Sewing Projects*. San Francisco: Chronicle, 2006.

Emerson, Jayne. *The Impatient Embroiderer*. New York: Potter Craft, 2006.

Ivarsson, Anna-Stina Lindén, Katarina Brieditis, and Katarina Evans. *Second Time Cool: The Art of Chopping Up a Sweater*. Buffalo: Annick, 2005.

McGrath, Jinks. *The Complete Jewelry Making Course*. Hauppage, N.Y. : Barron's, 2007.

Nicolay, Megan. *Generation T: 108 Ways to Transform a T-Shirt*. New York: Workman, 2006.

WEBSITES

www.sewing.org
If you love sewing, this is the site for you! There are a host of different clothing and craft projects for you to try.

www.wipapercouncil.org/makepaper.htm
A site that teaches you how to make recycled paper.

www.origami-club.com/en/
This site has lots of ideas for things to make using origami. These are demonstrated with either diagrams or animation.

www.learntoknit.com
This site has instructions and help with knitting.

www.nexstitch.com
This website offers simple videos demonstrating crochet stitches.

www.scrapbooking101.net
Find out more about scrapbooking.

ORGANIZATIONS

American Craft Council

72 Spring Street

6th floor

New York, New York 10012-4019

www.craftcouncil.org

This is the national organization for contemporary crafts in the United States. The council provides support for craftspeople, in addition to running training programs and staging events and exhibitions where craftspeople can exhibit and sell their products.

Metropolitan Museum of Art

1000 Fifth Avenue at 82nd Street

New York, New York 10028-0198

www.metmuseum.org

This great museum is a "must visit" for anyone interested in art and crafts. Check out the website to find out more about the museum's huge collections of beautifully crafted artifacts that include textiles, fashion through the ages, jewelry and accessories, ceramics, glassware, and metalwork.

Glossary

artificial made by people (the opposite of "natural")

artisan person who does skilled work with his or her hands

batik method of making patterns on cloth using wax and dye

batting soft material used for stuffing or padding

blended mixed together

bobbin part of a sewing machine on which thread may be wound to be used to sew

collage art form in which materials such as paper, cloth, or string are stuck onto a surface

complementary things that work together in a useful or attractive way

currency money of a country

customize make or change something

embellishment something added to make an object more beautiful or interesting

enamel glass-like paint that forms a shiny surface when dry

grain natural patterns in the surface of paper, wood cloth, and so on

graphic related to drawing or printing

iridescent having bright colors that change when moved

linen strong cloth that is woven from the fibers (thread-like material) of a plant called flax

matte surface color or paint that is not shiny

medium material used in art or crafts

memorabilia objects that are collected because they are connected with a person or event

natural fiber thread-like material made from plant or animal products

newsprint cheap, low-quality paper used to print newspapers

opaque something that light cannot shine through

parchment high-quality paper made to look like old fashioned parchment that was made with the thin, dried skin of animals

primary color one of three colors— which in paint, for example, are red, yellow, or blue—that can be mixed together to make any other color

proportion number or size of something when compared to the whole

secondary color color made by mixing together primary colors

semi-precious stone shaped piece of stone or rock used for making jewelry that is not valuable enough to be a gemstone, such as a diamond or a ruby

silk delicate, soft fabric made from a thread made by silkworms

slip knot type of knot that is easily untied and that forms a loop that can be made smaller or bigger

souvenir something you buy or keep to remember a vacation or special event

tie-dye method of making patterns in cloth using string, knots, and dye

versatile can be used in many different ways

Index